I feel sa

WAYLAND

Your Emotions

I feel angry
I feel frightened
I feel jealous
I feel sad

First published in Great Britain in 1993
by Wayland (Publishers) Ltd

This edition published in 2013 by Wayland,
an imprint of Hachette Children's Books

Hachette Children's Books,
338 Euston Road, London NW1 3BH

Wayland is a division of Hachette Children's Books,
an Hachette UK company
www.hachette.co.uk

Series editor: Mandy Suhr

British Library Cataloguing in Publication Data
Moses, Brian,
I feel sad. - (Your Emotions Series)
I. Title II. Gordon, Mike III. Series
152.4

ISBN 978-0-7502-1406-3

Typeset by Wayland (Publishers) Ltd
Printed in China

20 19 18 17 16

I feel sad

Written by Brian Moses

Illustrated by Mike Gordon

WAYLAND

When I'm sad I feel like...

a flower that
needs watering...

a rainbow that has lost its colours...

a clown who can't smile.

5

When I feel sad I lie on my bed. I don't want to speak to anyone...

I hide in the playhouse...

I cuddle my teddy.

All sorts of things make me sad. When my best friend moves to another house that's far away from me, I feel sad.

I promise I'll write.

But it will be exciting to get
lots of letters.

When my dog isn't well and the vet says,

He's getting very old you see.

I feel sad.

10

But I remember all the fun we've had together.

When Mum and Dad
argue and I hear loud
voices drift up the stairs
at night, I feel sad.

But the next day they're smiling and happy again.

When I'm saying goodbye to Gran at the railway station, and I know I won't see her for a while we both feel sad.

So I give her an extra long cuddle.
That makes us both feel better!

When all my friends are invited to a party except for me, I feel sad and left out.

So I give all my toys
a birthday party
instead!

Now, who
wants
ice-cream?

When I've painted a really good picture at school and then someone spoils it, I feel sad and a bit cross!

But next time I'll paint one that's even better.

When I find myself feeling sad it helps
if I tell my troubles to Grandad.

It helps if I do a jigsaw or watch something funny on television.

It helps if I have something to look forward to.

It helps if I can do something nice for someone else.

But sometimes the things I do can make other people sad...

if I call people names...

or if I'm rough
and don't take
enough care.

If I say things I don't mean, it can make Mum or Dad sad.

If I leave a friend out of my
game it can make him sad.

If you've been upset
and sad for a while,
turn your frown upside-down
and see it smile!

Notes for parents and teachers

Read the book with children either individually or in groups. Question them about how they feel when they're sad. Which of the ideas on page 4 is the closest to how they feel, or do they picture their sadness in different ways? Ask them to illustrate how they feel.

How do children behave when they're sad? Help them to compose short poems where each line begins, 'When I'm sad...' When I'm sad, nothing seems fun anymore/when I'm sad the sky is always grey/when I'm sad... Suggest that they think about other family members, friends, neighbours, teachers - what makes them sad and how do they show their sadness? Think also about how different people try to cheer themselves up - never mind, have a cup of tea; oh well, let's go out and enjoy ourselves, and so on.

Much of the book deals with the kind of situations that make children feel sad. Ask them to add to these and then to think of one situation that always makes them feel sad. Explain what happens and why. Who is responsible for the situation? What positive measures might be taken to make them feel less sad? This might be a good opportunity to talk about the local environment - a pond filled with rubbish, a litter strewn beach, a vandalized playground - would these things make children feel sad or angry or both?

Talk about other words that we use to describe being sad - unhappy, upset, miserable, tearful, gloomy, glum, dismal, unsmiling, etc. What do children understand by such phrases as - heavy hearted, sorry for oneself, sunk in the gloom, long in the face, down in the dumps, etc. Children may enjoy illustrating these ideas in an amusing way.

Discuss how our own behaviour affects others. Ask children to talk or write about the things that they do which make other people sad. Are there ways in which their own behaviour might change in order to avoid this effect on others?

Explore the notion of sadness further through the sharing of picture books and poems mentioned in the book list.

The above ideas will help to satisfy a number of attainment targets in the National Curriculum for English at Key Stage 1.

Books to read

Granpa by John Burningham (Red Fox). A small girl, her beloved granpa and the wonderful memories he leaves with her when he dies.

Dogger by Shirley Hughes (Picture Lions). Dave is sad when he loses his soft brown toy dog.

My Friend Whale by Simon James (Walker Books). A young boy has a blue whale for a friend but their friendship ends when the whale disappears.

A Very First Poetry Book compiled by John Foster (OUP). Includes the poem 'Sad Things' by Julie Holder.